AF365622

Garden of the Soul

Aaima K

BookLeaf
Publishing
India | USA | UK

Garden of the Soul © 2022 Aaima K

All rights reserved.

No part of this publication may be reproduced, stored in a retrieval system, or transmitted, in any form or by any means, electronic, mechanical, photocopying, recording or otherwise, without the prior written permission of the presenters.

Aaima K asserts the moral right to be identified as author of this work.

Presentation by *BookLeaf Publishing*

Web: www.bookleafpub.com

E-mail: info@bookleafpub.com

ISBN: 9789357446518

First edition 2022

Garden of the Soul © 2022 Aaima K

All rights reserved.

No part of this publication may be reproduced, stored in a retrieval system, or transmitted, in any form or by any means, electronic, mechanical, photocopying, recording or otherwise, without the prior written permission of the presenters.

Aaima K asserts the moral right to be identified as author of this work.

Presentation by *BookLeaf Publishing*

Web: www.bookleafpub.com

E-mail: info@bookleafpub.com

ISBN: 9789357446518

First edition 2022

DEDICATION

I dedicate this work to my parents - whose sacrifices have brought me here. Who lost their parents so I may have mine. Who miss their siblings, so they may raise mine.

ACKNOWLEDGEMENT

I would like to acknowledge the traditional custodians of Australia, whose turmoil precedes my residence in the land.

PREFACE

May you find a fragment of my soul which resonates with piece of yours.

Wilting Again

As the stars cling
To the sky's embrace

Hold me close
While I fall from grace.

In This Garden

Petals fall as flowers bloom,
Yet the trees forgive the passing of time.
Light glows where darkness looms,
Is it just nature in this world of mine?

Life is a brief spark,
Yet I still lament the length of it.
This garden is not just a park,
Where thorns are kept to the side and snipped.

As the universe grows,
And history repeats,
How shall I know if seeds which I sow
Are the ones I will reap?

As sure as time,
As clear as the sky,
This garden is not mine,
But still, I try.

And Yet, We Run

Breathless,
As tears well in your eyes,
When did this become your fault?

A race,
Where you are the sole runner,
Why do you refuse to stop?

What is your destination?
Death awaits us all,
Is that when you will halt?

'Rest is for the weak,'
The words which taint your lips, it seems
Your mind still rules your pace.

Unexpected turns break your speed.
When this race ends,
What starter will you face?

Australia

Where the spirit of the Earth,
Fills the veins of the rivers.
Where the sand of the dunes,
Remains warm beyond weathers.

Where September calls forth Spring,
And December beckons the heat.
Where fire holds birth,
And wildlife is its own feat.

Where blood stains the soil,
With centuries of sin.
Where rage fills the eyes,
Of those without my skin.

Where hate runs as deep,
As the roots of the youngest tree.
But, where love grows in blossoms,
Breathing from the old with history.

Short-lived and smelling sweet,
Lingering between the sour words.
The comforting air,
Which gives flight to the land's own birds.

Though the cities may reject,
My skin, my tongue, my faith.
The land will accept,
And those, in death, it will take.

Despite the dry winters,
And the stinging words of man.
This country is my home,
And I'll live as I can.

Seasons

Seasons change,
People come and go.
Winter melds into Spring,
A fact we all know.

But who could have known,
Of the pain I'd swallow,
Greeting the next Summer,
Knowing your soul won't follow.

To a Love Unknown

O you,
Whom I've yet to meet,
How kind is this world,
Which sits beneath our feet.

For you see the same sky,
Which I long for,
With a sigh.

For you praise the same saint,
Who suspends the stars,
And moon in the night.

The very master of time,
Who lifts the sun from its bed,
And raises it high for light.

If the moon were to break,
Or the stars were to fall,
I wonder, if then,
Would I meet you at all?

Let the moon break,
Let the stars fall,
Let the very thing that holds you back,
Be no more.
If that is what it takes,
To find your embrace,

Then I will let the world,
Make that sacrifice.

O you,
Whom I've yet to find,
Until your hands fill mine,
Until your smile meets my eyes,

The stars remain frozen,
The moon will still rise,
As if even they,
Await our time.

Spring Will Come Again

As the flowers which bloomed,
Begin to wilt

Know that they,
Who once stood still

Will return with grace,
Within the chill.

Metamorphasis

Change is a constant,
But it doesn't come gradually.

Change is a promise.
Meeting us inevitably,

Like the butterfly,
Emerging from a chrysalis.
Or the bloom,
Sprouting with catharsis.

Change meets us,
In times least expected.

Just as the pupa,
Squirms and disintegrates.
Just as the bud,
Fights the chill to germinate.

Let the struggle embrace you,
Use the challenge to guarantee,
The 'you' that is due
Surely, to set you free.

Promise

When stars collided,
And God decided
To put you before me.

I thought of a promise:
'Verlity,
Before the sky met the sea,
Your life was written
Perfectly.'

Dear Mumma

As the moon loves the Earth.
As the stars love the sky.

As winter years for spring.
As the sea clings to the shore's side.

As certain as the sun's rise in the east,
And its rest in the west.

My longing for you is greater,
Than the holds of nature's best.

But if the moon breaks,
Or the stars begin to fade.

When spring refuses to bloom,
Amid the winter's aches.

When the sun rises,
From where it did rest.

And the sea no longer kisses
the shore it knew best.

I will still reach out for you,
As when you held me to your chest.

Our Stories Are Our Own

Branches woven heedlessly,
Leaves growing from the knit.
The tree of life which grows our fate,
Is overripe with it.

Yet, within the fray,
Of seven-billion fates,
The gardener wrote a play.

Placing you in centre-stage,
With props in your way.
Asking you to dance to a tune,
That none of the others may.

Divinely Beloved

O you, with a heart of gold,
Little do you know
Of the power which you hold.

Your strength is so great,
That even the stars change their place,
So that they, too, my fit
Within this path you pave.

The moon,
Whose phases control the tide,
Even lingers, times at noon,
For the chance to meet your eyes.

For one so divinely loved,
Whose pain is shared with life,
You lower yourself too much,
Oh, what a dreadful sight.

When night turns to day,
And death's promise calls,
I hope you'll see how,
Upon seeing your grave,
Even planets will bow.

Home

I live as a stanger,
In the land of my childhood.
Seen as a foreigner
Where I feel I've always stood.

My wardrobe splits,
Two different cultural schemes.
One is 'normal',
The other 'obscene'.

My feet often long,
To stand where I was born.
My lungs often weep,
For the breath they first formed.

My heart holds fear,
That it might never know,
The place the people 'here',
Claim is my home.

Scapegoat

If praying in your place,
Would absolve you of your sins,
I would take up that task,
Regardless of my whims.

Autumn

The leaves fall,
As summer bids us once more.
The flowers breathe,
The sun does not scorch them anymore.

The air has a chill,
One we have begged for,
For the heat was too still.

The asphalt is cool,
The concrete,too.

The only thing unchanged,
Is this heart of mine,
Which still beats within.

Creation

Believe that you are as great,
As the mountains,
As the lakes.

Believe your place is true,
Like the sun,
Or Earth's moon.

Believe in your legacy,
For the one who made you,
Is the same who made this galaxy.

Creation was a promise,
And death is one too.
As you will face its kiss,
Know that mountains will wilt with you.

Love of the Land

This land loves man,
As the sun love the sky.
Nature craves your hand,
When you briefly pass by.

Mountains sing upon your birth,
And lakes weep upon your death.
The land is ablaze for your sins,
And the wind feeds your breath.

Crops lay themselves,
A sacrifice for your comfort.
Animals fall to your will,
For you, alone, are their master.

Clown Country

This is Clown Country,
Where they aim to please.
Unfortunately,
Not for the masses' ease.

Grey eminence runs the show,
Regardless of the figurehead –
They feel no need to know,
Just like those to be led.

Coal is beloved,
Rain is desired.
Fires run wild,
And disasters aren't mild.

But, this is Clown Country,
Where boats are turned away,
Children suffer,
But that doesn't matter, hey?

Poverty still strikes,
Within the land itself.
But that's a matter for the individual.
They brought it on themselves.

Land is plenty,
The people are few.
Cities reign empty,
Oh, what a view.

This is Clown Country,
Where they first look in their own backyard.
But what a shame,
That they don't want to work that hard.

This is Clown Country,
Where the land's most esteemed,
Are the corrupt minority,
With eyes only for greed.

Shooting Stars

Stars could fall,
And I would gather them all,
To place at your feet.

To give you countless wishes,
Hoping that they may replace
The control you seek.

No matter how great the sin,
Or how they would burn my skin,
I would endure it for your peace.

But regardless of my cries,
You would turn with a smile so wry,
And say my sacrifice was weak.

Serendipitous

There is no such thing as a coincidence.
The world was prepared with the precedence,
That you would exist,
And become a force to be reckoned with.

Prisoner

Once, I asked my soul;
'Why is it death that you crave?'

Her answer was soft, but bold.
'This life is a prison that God has made.'